BRAIN GAMES®

STICKER BY LETTER™

MAZES
IN THE WILD

Instructions

How to do STICKER BY LETTER™ MAZES

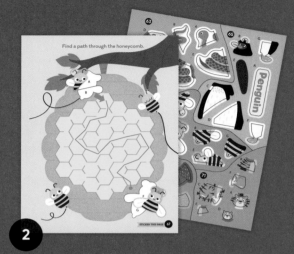

1 Pick your page and complete the maze. Start at the arrow and end at the dot.

2 If the page says STICKER THIS PAGE, find the stickers for that page number in the back of the book. Place the sticker with the same letter onto the matching space.

Louis Weber, CEO
Publications International, Ltd.
8140 Lehigh Ave
Morton Grove, IL 60053

Images from Shutterstock.com. Additional illustrations from Carles Ballesteros and Vanessa Port.

Permission is never granted for commercial purposes.

ISBN: 978-1-63938-527-0

Manufactured in China.

8 7 6 5 4 3 2 1

Let's get social!
- @Publications_International
- @PublicationsInternational
- @BrainGames.TM
- **www.pilbooks.com**

A

B C D E

Swim through this maze to find the way out.

Uh-oh: Help this sneaky racoon find the way through the maze.

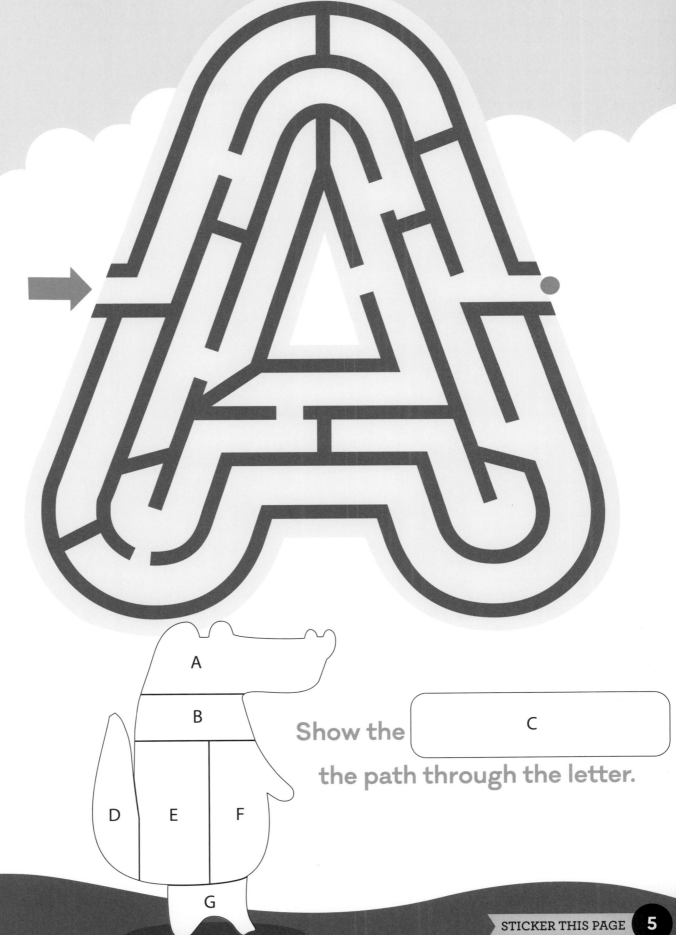

Show the C
the path through the letter.

Something smells good!
Show the mouse the way to this tasty snack.

A B C

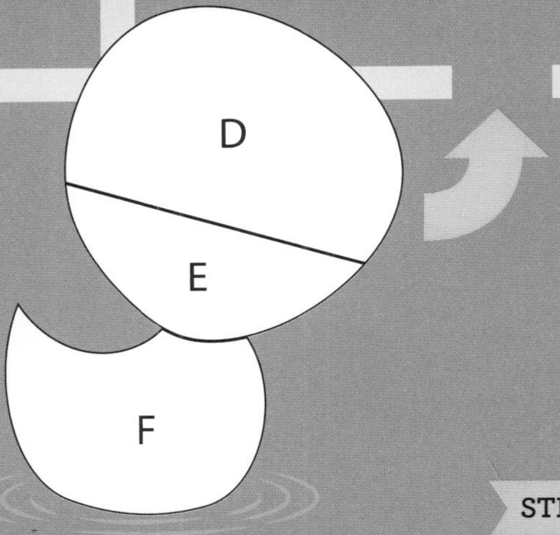

Reunite this mom with her babies by finding the right path.

D
E
F

Slither through this maze to find the end.

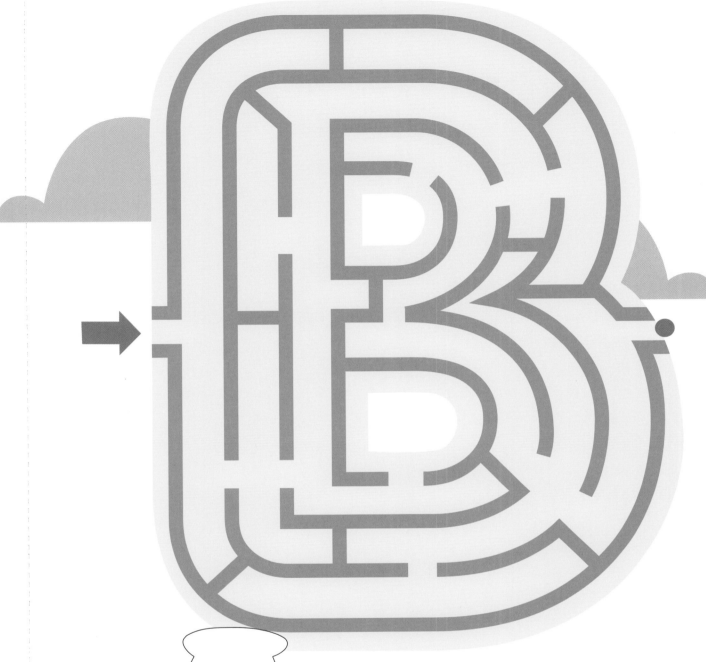

Find a path through the letter
for the [D].

Help this little fish find the way to join his friends.

Find the path
to the igloo.

Which path leads to the green dot?

Show the [A] the way through the letter.

The babies are waiting for their mom. Show her the way.

Find the way to reach the top.

Spot lost his friends at the dog park.
Can you help him find them?

16

Find a path through the letter for the E .

Help the monkey find the bananas.

There's only one way out!

Find the way
to the dot.

Show the

E

the way through the letter.

Be a sloth and take your time to find the way to the end.

Find a path to the food bowl.

TIGER

Help the baby goat climb up to its dad.

Help the C get through the letter.

Draw a path through the tiger's stripes.

Find a path to the mud puddle.

Help the chicks find the hen.

Help the [B] get through the letter!

This guy is hungry!
How can he get to his bowl?

Don't monkey around!
Find the path to the pink dot.

Show this sea star the way to its friends.

Help the [A] get through the letter.

Fly through the maze to join the others.

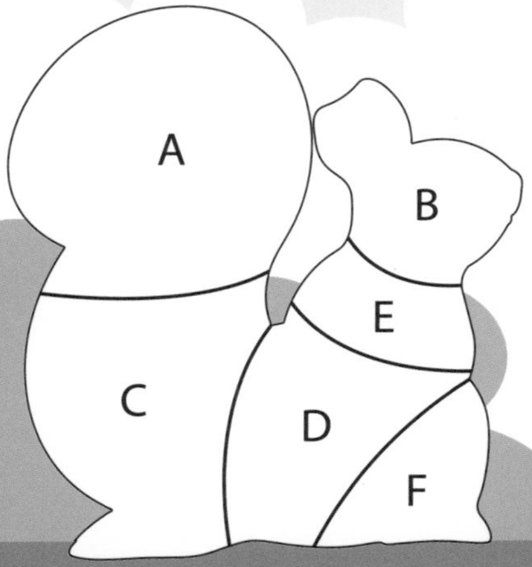

A

B

C

E

D

F

Help find the path to the nuts.

Can you see the way through this maze?

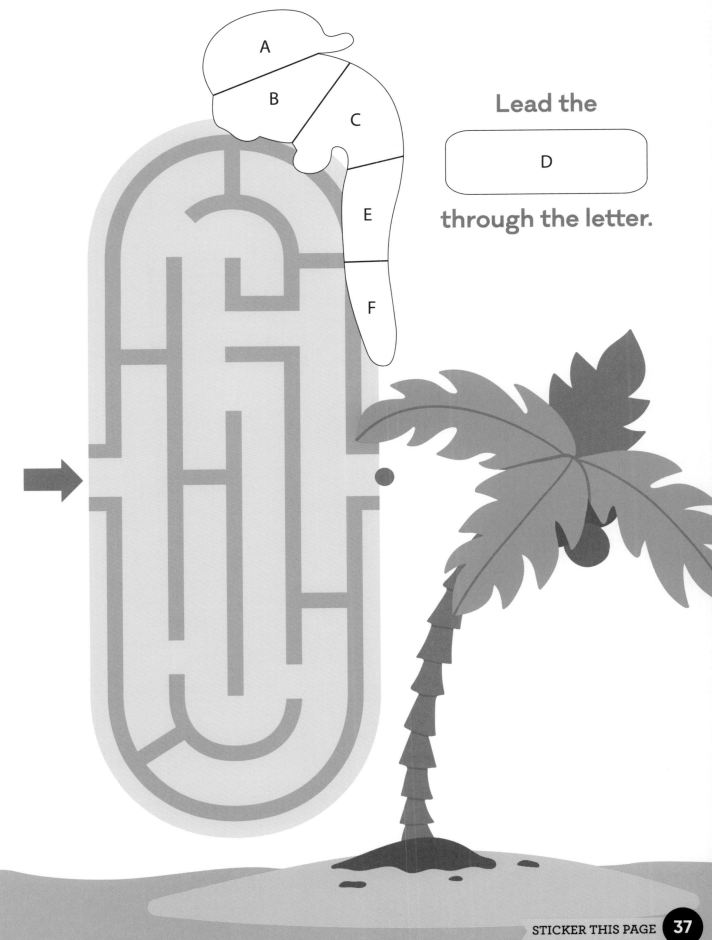

Lead the

D

through the letter.

Untangle the polar bears' fishing lines to find who caught the fish!

Find a path through the shell.

Can you find the way to the palm trees in the middle?

Guide the [A] through the letter.

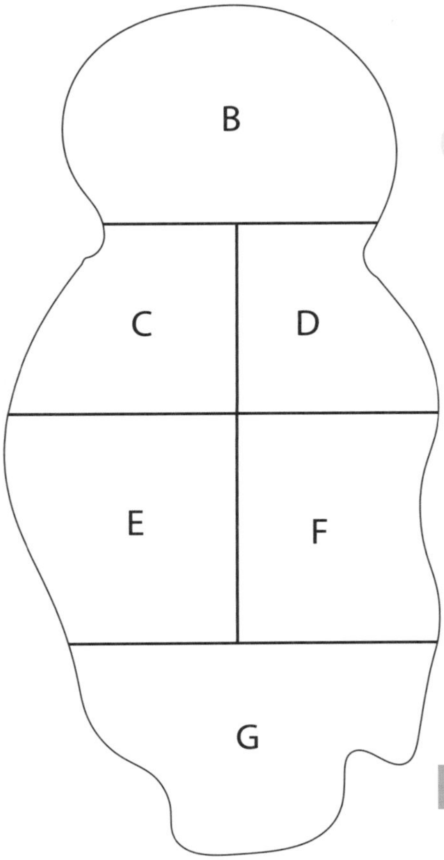

B

C | D

E | F

G

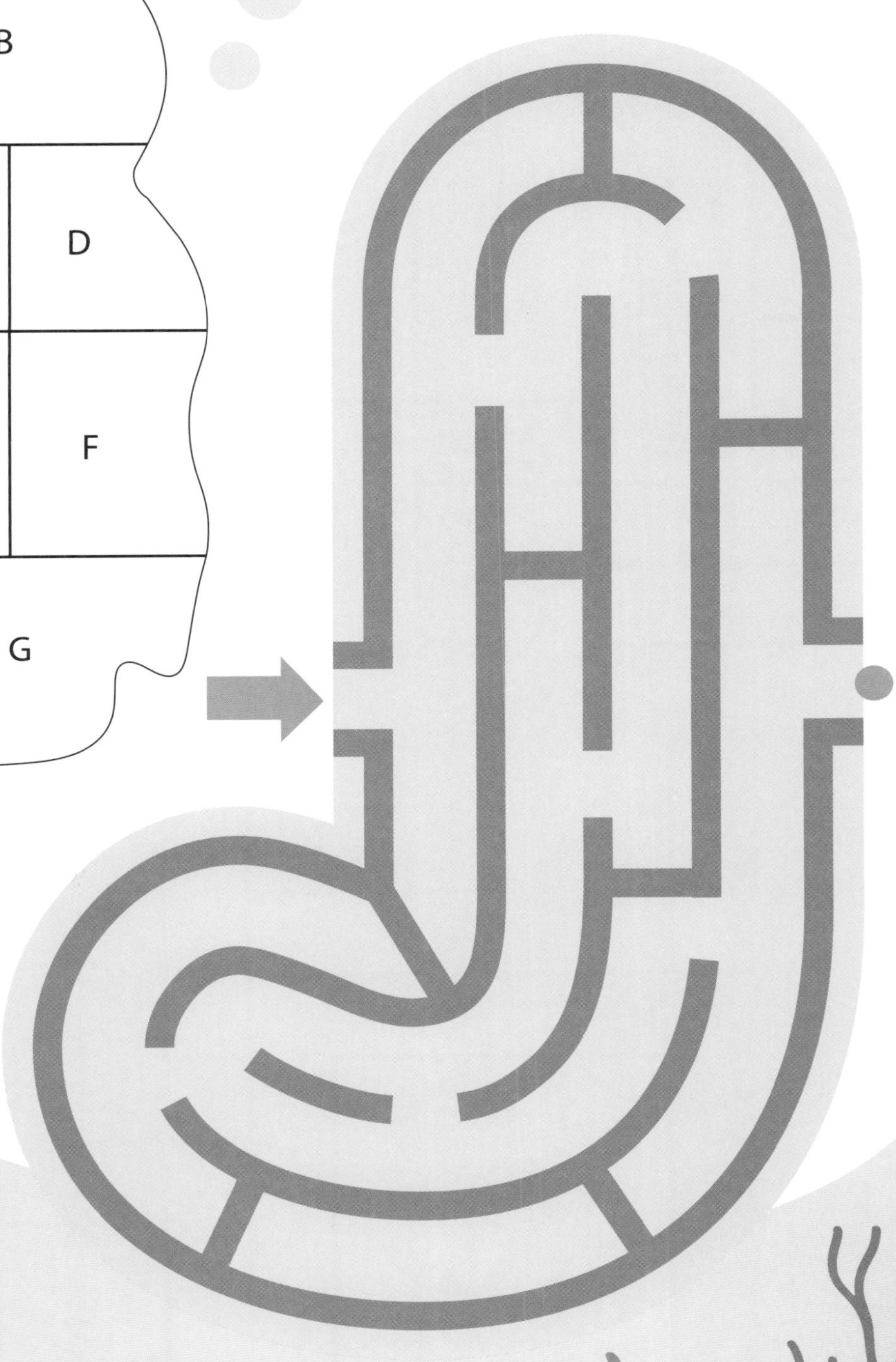

Get bzzzzy! Guide this bee to the hive.

Help the animals choose the right way to get to the lake

Draw a line from the sheep to the other animals.

44

Show the [A] the path through the maze.

Time to get to the barn!
Which is the right way?

Help find the right path through the maze!

A
B
C
D

E
F

Find a path through
the peacock's feathers.

Find the path that leads to the [A].

It's a beautiful day in the garden. Help the butterfly find the flowers!

Find a path through the cave to find a friend!

A

B

C

D

E

Draw a line from the blue arrow to the blue dot.

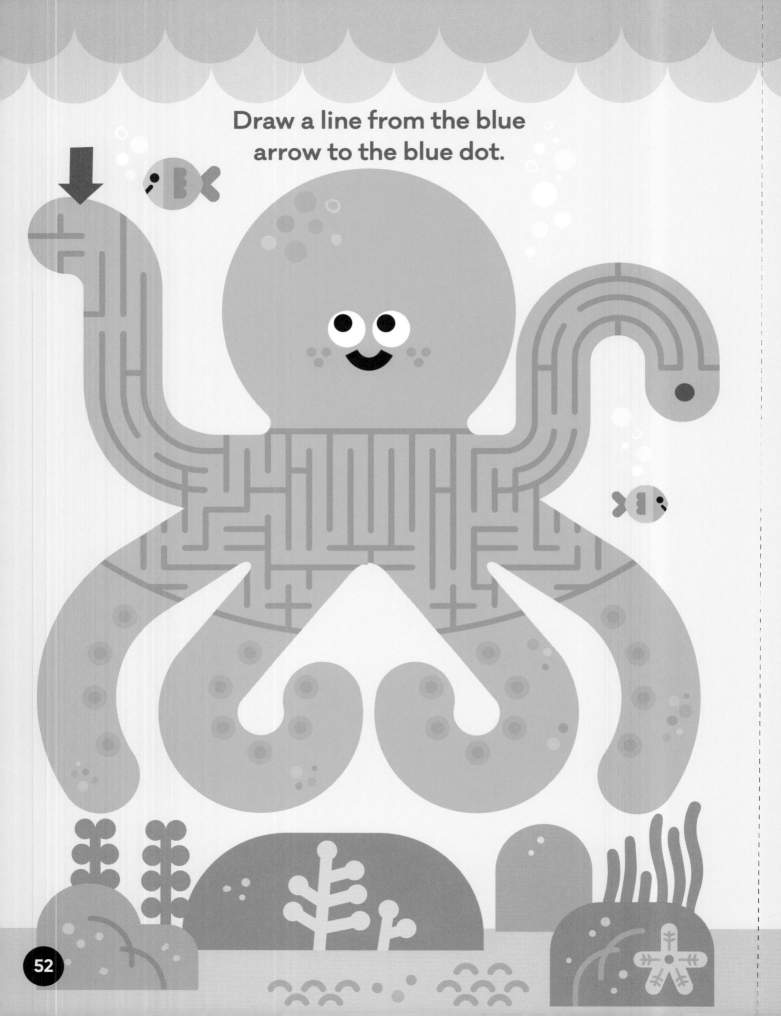

Help the [A] find a path through the maze.

Find a path across the turtle's shell.

A

B

C | D

E | F

Help find a path to the web.

It's cold up here!
Help the reindeer calf
find its parents!

Guide the [A] through the letter.

Time for a nap.
Which way leads to the cave?

58

Find a path to fly to the nest.

It's time to hide nuts for winter.
Help the squirrels find the trees!

Help the [A] find a path through the letter.

Sharks can't move backwards! Help it swim forward through the maze.

Draw the path through the maze.

A B

C

D

E F

Help the mole
find its burrow.

Find a path through the maze

for the [A] .

These little guys are waiting for lunch! Help mama find the way.

Find a path through the honeycomb.

There's only one way to the watering hole!

68

Draw a path through the letter for the

C .

Gophers are good diggers.
How can this gopher reach its den?

Find a path through the desert.

Hang out with this opossum and work the maze to find the red dot.

Help the C

find a path to the end of the maze.

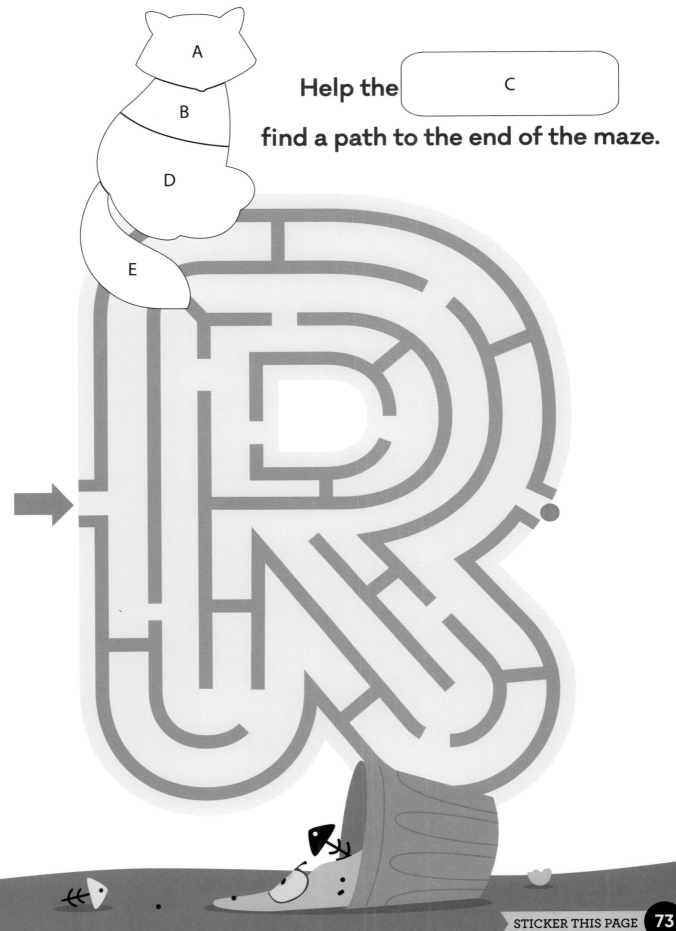

This frog would rather sit on a lilypad.
Can you find the way?

Find a path
through the maze.

This ostrich needs to check on her eggs.
How should she get there?

Lead the F through the letter.

Hop through the maze
to reach the red dot.

With so many nests, there's only one way to reach the end.

Crunch time! One way leads to the worm. Can you find it?

Show the ![A] the path through the maze.

Help the rabbit find its friend!

Go for a dig and find the bone!

Help the bear find a path through the maze.

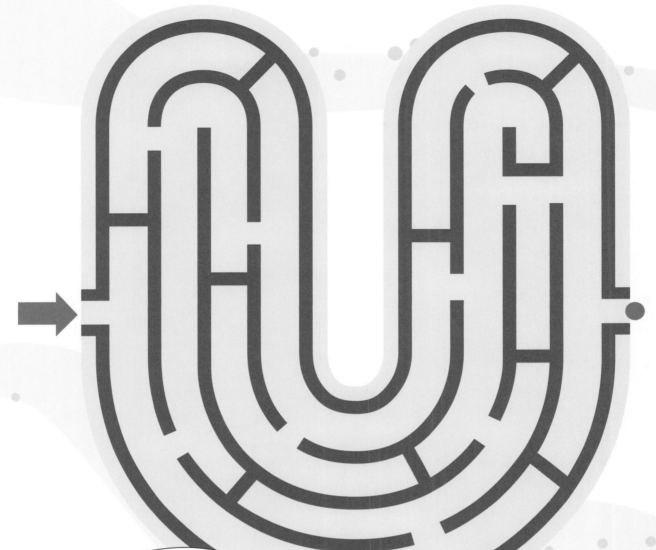

Find a path through the maze for the

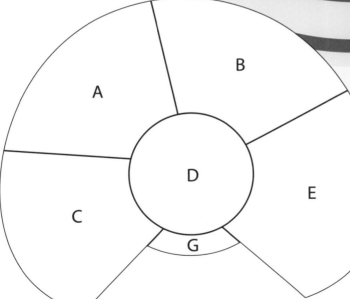

	F

Will you help the horse through the maze?

Find a path to the pond through the maze.

Find a path through the giraffe's spots.

Help the [C] choose a path through the maze.

Help the goats find a path
up the mountain!

Show the [A] the path through the letter.

B

C

D E F

Reunite these friends by finding the way through the maze.

Climb through the maze to find a friend!

A

B   C

D   E

F

G

Find a path through the maze.

94

Discover the path through the letter for the

B

.

A treasure
awaits if you can
find the correct path!

Guide the [A] through the maze.

B

C

D

E

F

Guide the penguin to his friends.

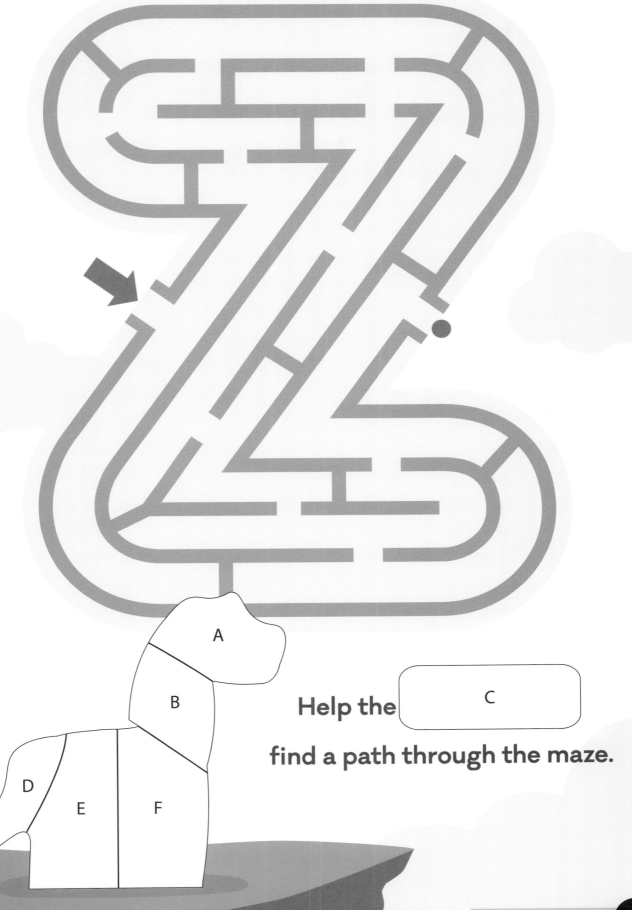

Help the [C] find a path through the maze.

page 3

page 4

page 5

page 6

page 7

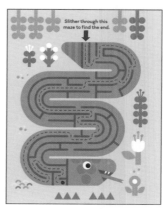
page 8

page 9

page 10

page 11

page 12

page 13

page 14

page 15

page 16

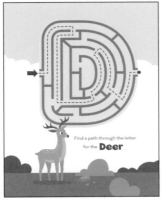
page 17

page 18

page 19

page 20

page 21

page 22

page 23

page 24

page 25

page 26

page 27

page 28

page 29

page 30

page 31

page 32

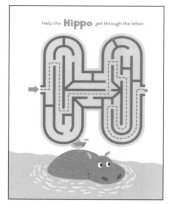
page 33

page 34

page 35

page 36

page 37

page 38

page 39

page 40

page 41

page 42

page 43

page 44

page 45

page 46

page 47

page 48

page 49

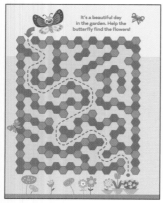

page 50

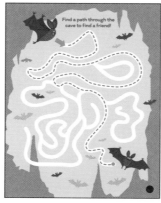

page 51

page 52

page 53

page 54

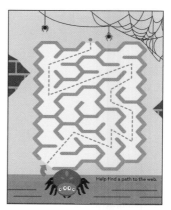

page 55

page 56

page 57

page 58

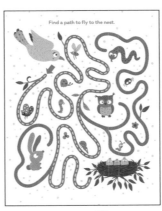

page 59

page 60

page 61

page 62

page 63

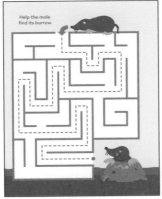

page 64

page 65

page 66

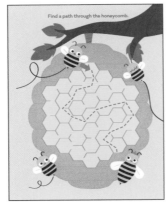

page 67

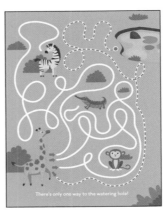

page 68

page 69

page 70

page 71

page 72

page 73

page 74

page 75

page 76

page 77

page 78

page 79

page 80

page 81

page 82

page 83

page 84

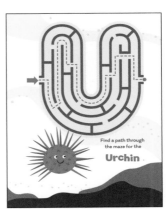

page 85

page 86

page 87

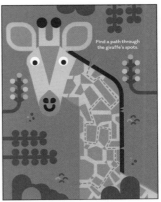

page 88

page 89

page 90

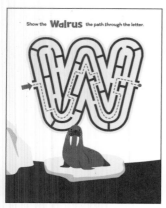

page 91

page 92

page 93

page 94

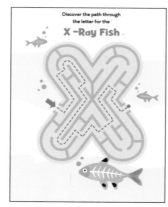

page 95

page 96

page 97

page 98

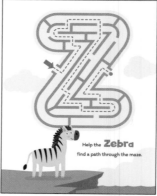

page 99

Alligator

Bear

13 Cow

15

17 Deer

19

21 Elephant

23
A
B
E
C
D

25
A
G
E
C
D
B
Fox
F

27
B
D
E
C
A

29
B
C
E
A
Giraffe
D
F

31
H
B
I
C
G
F
A
E
D

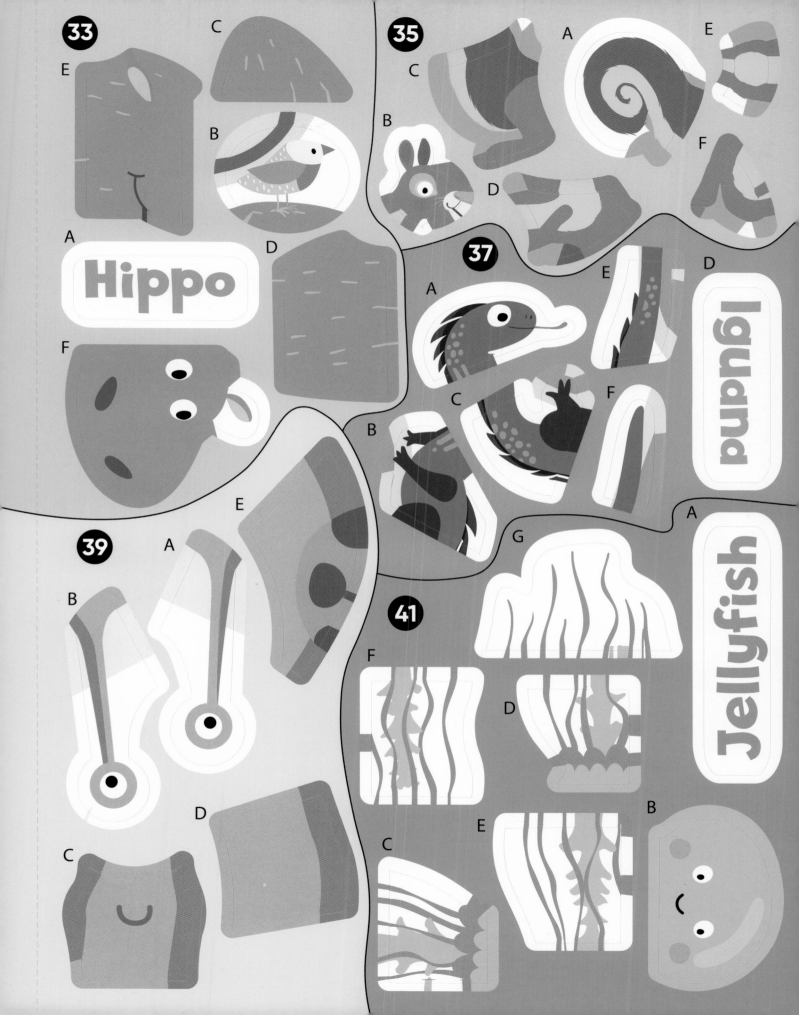

33

E C
B
A

Hippo

D
F

35

A
C
B
E
D
F

37

A
E
D
C
F
B
Iguana
G
A

Jellyfish

39

A
B
E
C
D

41

F
D
E
C
B

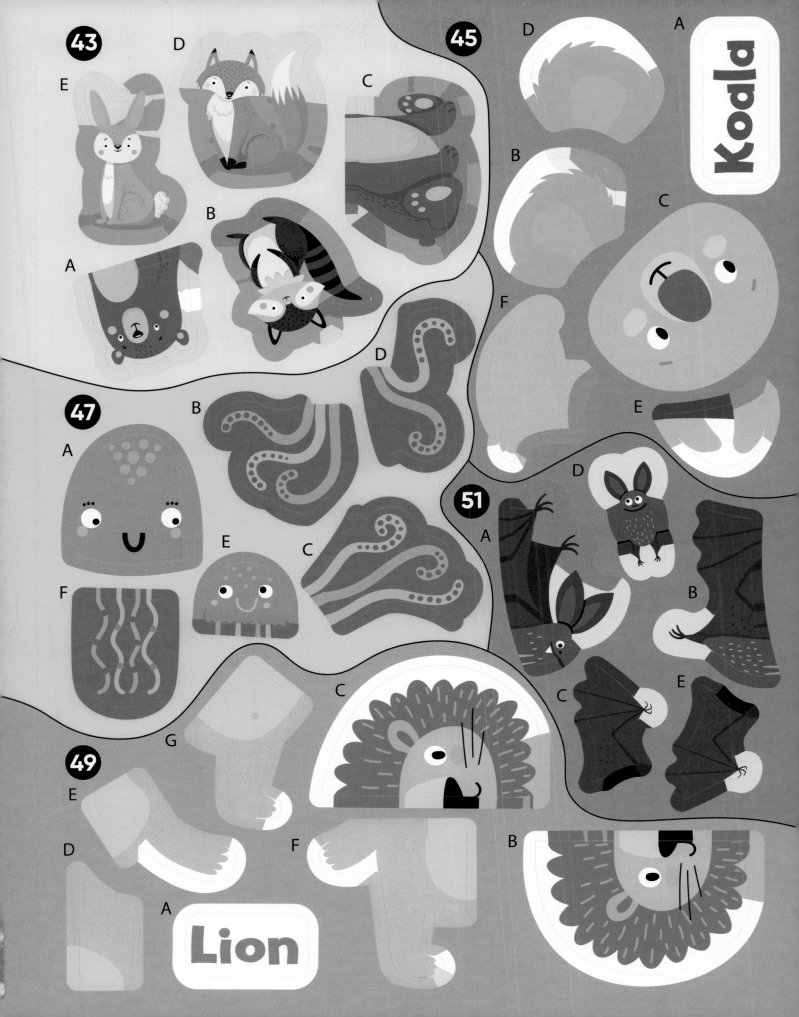

43
D
E
C
B
A

45
D
A
B
C
F
E

Koala

47
A
B
D
E
C
F
G
C

49
E
D
A
F
B

51
D
A
B
C
E

Lion

53 Monkey

55

57

59

61 Owl

Narwhal

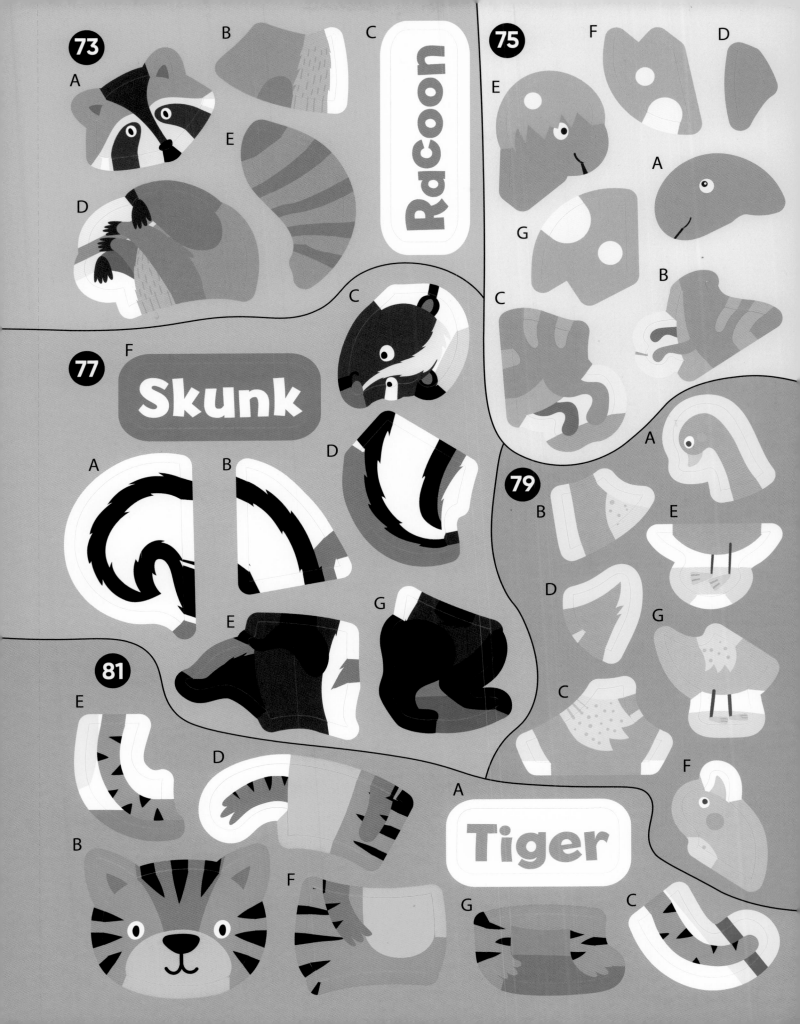

73
A B C
D E

75
F D
E
G A
B
C
A

Racoon

77
F C
Skunk
A B
D
E G

79
A
B
E
D
G
C
F
C

81
E
B
D A
F
Tiger
G C

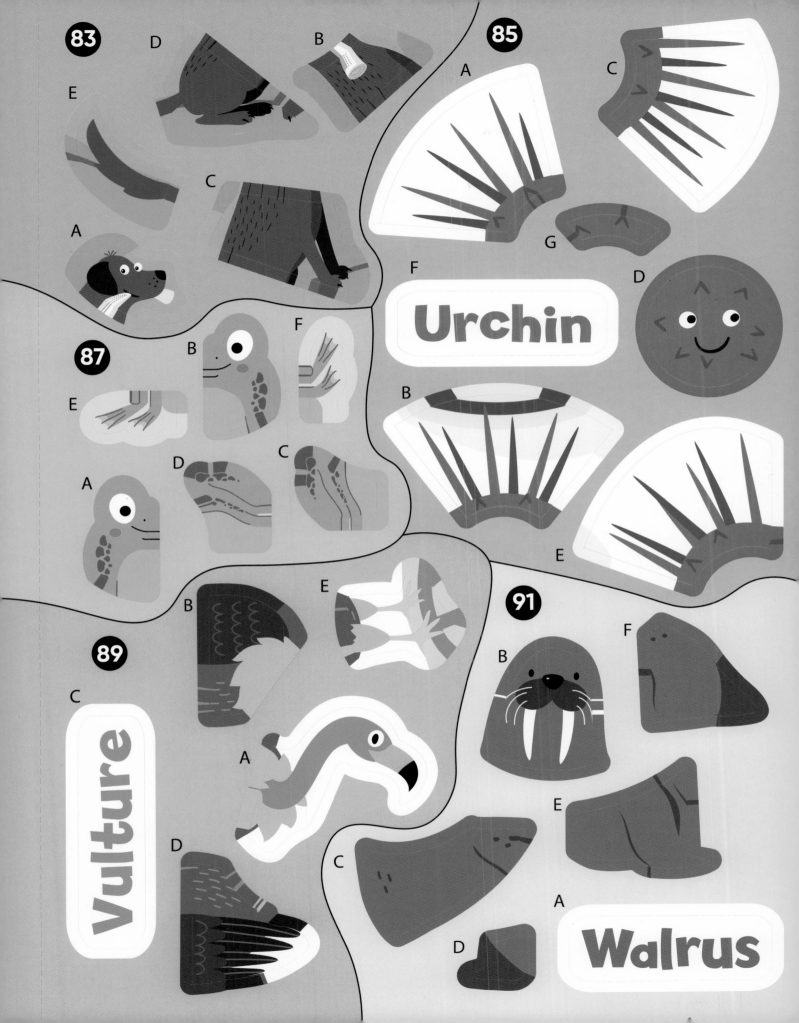

83

D
E
B
C
A

85
A
C
G
F **Urchin** D
B
E

87
B
F
E
A
D
C

89
Vulture
C
B
E
A
D

91
B
F
E
C
A
D
Walrus